Eighteen Glimpses

Daniela Estefania Cadena
Huerta

BookLeaf
Publishing

India | USA | UK

Presentation by *BookLeaf Publishing*

Web: www.bookleafpub.com

E-mail: info@bookleafpub.com

ISBN: 9789363308930

First edition 2024

PREFACE

My mama was born in Sinaloa, Mexico, where she lived with a family of at least ten until her early teens. At that time in her life, she was kicked out of her home and lived with extended family until early adolescence. During this period, she often found herself on the streets, struggling to survive against abuse, the blistering heat and freezing cold, scorpion stings, and filth.

She was pregnant with me at seventeen and had me at eighteen. Unlike me, with the privilege of attending college, my ma did not have the opportunity to finish even elementary school. She has worked to live since she was a child and has fought against many types of assault on her humanity that I cannot bring myself to name.

One of the most unfortunate aspects of life are the cycles that never seem to end, indifferent to who experiences them. Growing up a witness to the effects of life on my ma, I'd ask myself: why her? Why did she, with a visionary mind and a kindness that hasn't dissipated, have to endure the worst humanity had to offer? Why couldn't it have been someone who, I don't know, deserved it because they acted on their cruelest desires?

My ma prayed to God, went to church, expressed gratitude with a sincerity that taught me to live with that same level of appreciation, and showed sympathy to others as though she shouldn't have saved any for herself.

Of course, there is no straightforward answer to why bad things happen. They simply do, as I've learned through my own life experiences. However, there has remained one indisputable constant in my ma's life amidst all the changes she's endured. A force so powerful I couldn't help but write about it—loosely basing this collection on her life story in an attempt to replicate and understand her drive for life—my ma has carried with her a will like that of the sun, which rises every day.

I've never written poetry outside of school assignments, so this book—written for a writing challenge I haphazardly stumbled upon on the internet—will be neither perfect nor imperfect. Ultimately, it is up to you, the reader, to form the story and piece together your own opinions. However, at the end of this tale, I ask you to ponder a timeless question that I've struggled to understand for my mother, who was hardly given any: what is your reason for living?

Sincerely,
Daniela Estefania Cadena Huerta

Minute 1

Waves I splash with pleading silence,
My fingers, lungs, and rivers matched.
Touch so soft my skin shall rip,
Tell me, father, will this be my last?

Stranger with the angel's glare
Is what you see not to your prayer?
Eyes is muddy like ground I seek,
Burning red with salt you speak.

You're not like me, I'm not you
But still my hands grow cold
your white,
my lungs share the air
you breathe,
my teeth color the light
you see,
my veins the blue heavens
same ones we preach.

Stranger with the angel's glare,
a desperate air not enough for you.
Move away with dream police,
leave me to drown in peace.
Freedom is limited,

not enough for me.
So leave me,
leave me to drown in peace.

Minute 2

Green was your favorite color.
The bark on the trees, the shapes of sky itself
The leaves with embeds of stars and hopes,
You'd tell me, baby, Your wish.
Your wish in every tree I see now.

momma, i want to live where we see trees
where we walk on dirt with our bare feet
no painting ground a crying color
where our toes embraced by grass will love
grime of our own will
where me and you can pick red fruit
no iron taste to get it.

momma, You say to me.
where there are trees,
will there be me?

Minute 3

You is everywhere.
You is the light blinding eyes in the water,
the sound of laughing sadness when metal touch
the head,
the refreshing burn at the roof of my mouth,
the wind hollowing my gasps out.

momma, You say to me.
will i see a tree someday?

Yes, my Baby
For You is everywhere.
You in every tree I see now.
You in the shape of bark and leaves and
seaweed.
You in more green than you could have ever
dream.

Minute 4

momma had nice eyes
they'd see me with water
and water was cold,
not like mean sun.

momma had colored eyes
the only color in the house.
she did everything and
gave me the color red
to remember
because she said,
gray not good enough to be
my only color.

momma sometimes brought green home
green was my favorite
because she bring home
butter and bread
stories of heaven
wrinkles in face,
my rare treasures.

Minute 5

Clink-a-clank— scrap ceilings singing for rain,
muddying the world in unusual ways
was crying heaven, he who grew wonder
for the sand between my toes stuck like lovers,
the shine at the tippy-top of my head
aged without age— face that of the misled,
stolen smells: my sugarcane sickly sticky
sweet before the earthy taste seeped me shame.

Alike in lies was the bread-man, kind giver
of fluff when hunger stung taste buds bitter.
Alike in lies was the speaker, lessons
free with dirt ink: my A, B, C, D.
Alike in lies was ma's "him,"
heavy hand rusted all skin.

Ma would turn them away sneer on her face
Rule number one: nothing lasts free in this space
Not you not me not anybody, ma screamed
when ma's "him" bought and sell me.

Minute 6

You're a fool for pretending to have
a will, stupid and foolish and hopeless
as your moving legs are restrained the more you
move.
The more you move the more life grabs you
so stop the sting, apply some aloe, take it
with eyes closed (good girl)
new yoga pose (that's right)
as the americans call it.

Familiar! That's what the fire was,
in every branch of my lungs
lit and put out lit and put out.
Water gushing back and forth
Through coughing choking whimpering
Though no more scratching, kicking, crying.
Calmer rule 2.
Meditation, as the americans call it.
Foolish, as my mother called it.

Minute 7

Not even mud cookies
For roach begging eyes
For doggy sharp teeth
For swelling chests
Both of glee and tears
Your swelling stomach
Needs it more, right?
Ribs counting down like
A hungry hourglass
Longing for shivers
Of eyes undistilled by life
Why must we then,
if longing is to exist,
water it down, water it down
when it's unadulterated
pure, sweet goodness
love to keep going
hope to keep swimming
swimming even if mother said it was foolish and
stupid and hopeless,
swimming.

Minute 8

Swimming,
then there's land.

Flaxen hair with blessings from the sun's rays
Eyes a nourishing green unlike the world's
selfish greed, self-proclaimed nobility
whose hands hurt, not healed, rusted bloody skin
while his was a bath on a hellish day.

All free with a kindness unrepaid,
no needing to restrain my thighs with him
bathing in my thoughts with my asking, mine
my choice, my blessing, my willing to swim
my own rescue, my own running, my own
painting the ground red each step on hot sand
the fire of glass, scorpions, and ants
no match for the fire of him, hand out
for me, me, me.

He was a trickle of sweat one summer day,
expected, known of, unwanted until I saw
he was my savior.

Minute 9

He promised to come back, and he did so
with berries, bread, milk, juice, fruit, eggs, last
names,
no kindness of thighs worth the value of
my fireplace! Baking a joy of
no-more, no-less, no-longer.
No-more rusted skin, I declare
No-less food than what baby needs, I declare
No-longer not restraining, I declare
my stomach is mine, my love is mine, I love you
I declare.

Minute 10

His name will be Sol, I told him.
What was the saying? With butterflies in my
heart?
His cheeks rose I remember, wrinkled eyes
glowing.
Sol. Our son, my sun, my round declaration to
the world.
Loved from the moment he kicked, moved,
danced,
in my belly too fragile to caress.

Too fragile to caress, my savior said.
What was the saying? I was head over heels?
Yes, for he was so kind, too kind to touch me in
fear of breaking me, he said.
Breaking me! Never, not anymore. My mother
tried, "he" tried, but suns
always shine, no matter the time, and I shall rise,
rise, rise from soils depraved.

Too busy working for you, my love, he said.
What was the saying? He was the apple to my
eye?
He provided me the seed to my happiness, and
now he worked for me

he completed me, cured me, abstained me of sin.
My everything.
Dust grew softer with every visit of his to the
heaven
he built just for me,
Far away to keep me cool, he said. To keep me
safe.
What did I tell him again? All I needed was his
love, I said.

Minute 11

The rushing river descended from heaven
sour forbidden fruit allowing its entrance to open
with trumpets and choir echoing the arrival.
I shall take on your desires,
you won't need to be like me,
a wound upon this earth it's trying to hide.
Sing! Let your arrival be known,
I'll sing with you, through pain through
happiness
You'll be mine I'll be yours
You won't need no restraining,
You won't need no rescuing,
You're the sun, the ruler of you
your hands, your legs, your cries.
You're sticky, you're red, there's a red heart on
the ground,
Is it mine? Is my heart finally free?
You're sweet, you're warm, there's trees in your
eyes.
My sun, you brought the world you'll grow with
your arrival.

Minute 12

Our neighbor rats drank from your essence,
they squeaked your name my dearest. Your first
friends!
You held them as gently as your father held me
our first moon,
full of sincerity, a childish bliss I hadn't seen
ever.
Today, I picked up a book I stole from the
library,
in and out quickly, they didn't notice a thing
their A, B, C's are our treasure
It even has the rest of them, ones stolen from us!
Did you know E is for Elephant?
And F is for flower!
There are many more letters just for you, my
dearest
letters to spell out your world how you like it
And I'll be there to help you write it,
I'll be there with ink, and if there's none, we'll
prick my finger,
I'll be there with your paper, and if there's none,
I'll steal just for you.
Just for you, as your father did just for me.

Minute 13

I saw you today, my savior.
I saw you today, with your new plot.
I walked out of the alleyway,
I took a left to the vendedor on the street who
sells fruits,
I had no money of yours to give, but I had my
sun, and he gave me a bag of apples for free.
I thanked him for kindness my mother taught me
to ignore.
I walked down the street of our creaky town
bristling with sunday shoppers,
I saw you my savior, a bouquet of roses in hand.
Expensive.
I thought they were for me; that you knew we
were fated to meet as your eyes fated to love.
I was walking through a cloud of dreams. Legs
soft, back soothed, lips ready.
I saw you walk to someone else. They wore a
white dress and held a purse.
I'd never gotten to hold a purse or wear colors
like white.
She held the flowers you gave her and bowed
her head to smell them
She smiled at you with red
She let out air with a haha

She held the flowers tight
She leaned in
She leaned in
You leaned in
She wore a ring
You wore an identical ring
You smiled at her with your green eyes of
nurturing and trickery
I screamed,
I pray the flowers you gave to her rot
I condemn you my savior,
I have your son and your life which you gave to
me years ago
I will never forgive you.
You pretended I was crazy. Who was I?
I must be confused.
I must be a prostitute on drugs.
Poor kid.
You walked away.

Minute 14

You walked inside the home you built.
You're sorry, you wish you told me sooner, you
never meant it,
You always had a wife,
you've always wanted kids,
you've always loved me.

The words rang as hollow as the pit in my gut.
The words banged and clashed inside until they
changed shape.

You're a whore, you should have known,
You knew it was your job,
You were raised to be a parasite, now you won't
leave me be,
You ruined my life,
You don't know how to be a mother,
You're a disgrace to God
You're not human,
you you you you
you.

Minute 15

Shine split me awake
Throbbing truth numbing my touch
Must the sun go down?

Minute 16

I could hear you call my name at night.
Where were you taken? To a heaven just for
you?
Where you could spell your life with all the
letters
you could ever want and need?
Where you'll see trees so big and tall,
matching the caring green you got from me?
I was told where to look for you.
Go dream, I was told. And with money from
restraining my cries I found your dream.
Meet with the crow who will lead you to the
wolf who will lead you to the crocodile
go inside the crocodiles mouth and find the pearl
run with it until the pearl turns yellow.

I'll find you.
I'll be the one to show you trees and colors
I'll steal you books with all sorts of letters.

Again and again you locked me down
you ran me down from rock to dirt
Again and again.
Is my thirst for normalcy wrong?

Minute 17

You're just like me.
You stare with the same human eyes and human
flesh
With the same heart no one listens to, I wager.
Seaweed wraps along my legs,
Black straps wrap around your shoulders.
Your light shines in my face,
My eyes shine on your face.
Freedom is limited,
there's not enough for me,
won't you let me steal some happiness, sir?
Leave me be if the answer is no,
If my hunger for sanity is wrong.
If my desire to take on the desires of those who
need,
despite me always needing needing needing,
then leave me to rot like the flowers never given.
Allow me the grace to drown if God has deemed
me a disgrace.

Minute 18

You speak in letters unknown to me.
Choochoo cha, goud taday?
Your judgment calls upon an answer from me
That's strange.
Can you tell me when I asked for your pardon?
I'm the wound you're trying to hide,
the scar rated as forgettable to your world.
Seventeen years stinging you each scratch,
the scab ripped of again and again,
in this lonely world where sun was stolen.